CONTENTS

THE BLACK MAN

The color of my skin, thoughts and actions is called black. Sometimes I am detested, rejected, humiliated because of being black. If I may ask, "What is black?" It is a derogatory, dehumanizing or degrading term of reference; not just used to describe but to emasculate the man in me. It represents everything and anything negative, bad, wicked, corrupt and so on.

But, that is not me! Oh, no! That is not me!
The blackness in me is loud and proud!

History is enriched by my ancestors
Of lawyers, professors, doctors, inventors.
The list goes on like the River Nile
Overflowing the banks of civilization with knowledge, inspiration and sense of direction.

The chains no longer enslave but empower me to believe in myself and a power greater than myself. I am able to soar high above the walls of ignorance, stupidity and arrogance once considered the blackness in me.

I now embrace wisdom, knowledge and understanding with an open-mind, being imprisoned by the walls of passion and hunger to empower, enhance, inspire and contribute to a social change called- **"betterment of you and me."**

I am humbled not by the cat-of-nine tails anymore but, by the dignity, integrity and self-realization of who I am. I am powerful, intelligent, sensitive, kind among others. This is the road I tread upon, daily to exalt the blackness in me.

Like the statue of liberty, I stand tall and proud to protect,

Provide and preserve the nubian queens of my heritage. They sometimes may be called whores, bitches but, to me they are beautiful and full of grace and as such should be respected, loved, adored and appreciated.

I don't see the "white-man as my enemy" but the catalyst to change; I must change the way I think, act and thereby empower not only the color of my skin but the content of my character.

MY NUBIAN SISTA

Hold high your head above the waters
Of ignorance, arrogance and stupidity
and stand firm upon the principles
Of love, peace and integrity
The fabric of your identity.

Don't subject yourself
To vulgarity, idiosyncrisy or hypocrisy
But to solidarity, honesty and dignity
Precepts often overlook by our society.

Compromise not the woman in you
Of substance, class and authority
And though you are strong, black and independent
We need each other for growth and development.

Be a fountain of knowledge, wisdom and understanding
To your offspring, of the struggles, deaths and dreams
Of men and women-pioneers of your history
Like footprints on the pages of humanity.

Your beauty is like sunshine by day
And moonlight by night
Radiantly shining, ever so bright
Holding me captive to this awesome sight!

As the mother of civilization
You provide the strength and inspiration
We all need in the darkest hour
Like the rock of Gibraltar.

Don't perpetuate the inferiority complex of the past
Bestowed upon you like the lonely, withering grass
But, stand tall and proud like The Sears Tower
Empowering your man, sister or brother.

TEARY EYES

The Teary eyes I can't hide
Birth from pains down deep inside
Bring to life, those history scenes
When we weren't considered human-beings.

The vicious dogs as they rushed and barked
Were the white-man's eyes within the dark
For as the bullets hit like spear
Our lives were shattered in despair.

See the kids being ripped away
From mother's arms without delay
And fathers emasculated before their eyes
While screams of "rape" echoed from their wives.

Hear the houses crumbling down
As they scorched and burnt to the ground
For even the fields, they too died
From the raging, fiery, angry tide.

So lost and confused was our world
Being stripped of life as we twisted and twirled
For even with the chains enslaved
Thousands found an early grave.

Many a nights, teardrops were our friend and company
While fear became our bed of agony
How excruciating was our daily life
Being confronted by heart-aches and strife.

The flight from plight and misery
Still distorts our true history
For as a people-so strong and full of vitality
Knowledge and dignity
The pictures painted are not our reality!

The struggles and sacrifices we have faced
Have empowered and enriched us with grace
To soar beyond the walls of idiosyncrisy
And overcome the hurdles of hypocrisy.

THE EMASCULATED MAN

Beneath the chains of oppression
Manifests the birth of the emasculated man
Journeying through this society
Struggling to regain his identity.

Stripped of his innate qualities
Disempowering him via the forces of government
Is subjected to manifest compliancy and humility
Otherwise confronts degradation or imprisonment.

No longer his mandatees are respected
Nor his values adhered to
For the empowerement of the woman has rejected,
undermined and castrated what the man can do.

The social constructs dehumanize such image
Leaving him frustrated and lost in vision
The ability to provide, protect and discipline in age
Is overtaken by the woman or nation.

The homes become basically matriarchal
Leaving the fathers powerless or absent
Thereby reversing the roles for all
With mothers becoming men at present.

Despite statistics on abandonment or imprisonment
The repurcussions have led to identity confusion
Due to lost of self-actualization and disempowerment
Igniting a global upheaval of epic proportion.

Overcoming these struggles, hurdles and so forth
Man and woman must consolidate their efforts
To realign, enrich and empower each other
Thereby crushing the head of the vampire.

AMERICA'S CHANGE

The metamorphosis of America's moral values
Has deconstructed the fabric of its existence
By diluting and dehumanizing the fundamental dues
That should be given to life in its reverence.

Its insensitivity and acceptance of such transition
Are in dire need of radical intervention
The absence of sound principles governing a nation
Ultimately climaxes into self-destruction.

The acceptance of wrong becoming right
And right becoming wrong, morally,
Has birth the concept of "normality" into light
That has undermined its dogmas naturally.

Its influential power, globally,
Is the venom which poisons this world
That epitomizes this nation's functionality
Despite its military and economic twirl.

The forces and instruments of change
Hide themselves behind the arms of the law
By manifesting and justifying a derange
Inconsiderate, negative and destructive flaw.

How often has the tentacles of injustice
Victimize, immoralize, dehumanize your society
Within the framework of this,
A thought she calls "national security."

In pursuit of life, justice and liberty
The fundamental principles of this society
Ironically, we are victims of their creation
Having defeated the purpose of this nation.

THE VOICE

The voice of his ancestors
Cries from beneath the earth
As the struggles and oppression flow
like teardrops
Upon the face, cheeks and tongue of
his birth.

See the magnitude of pain and anger
Erupt like a violent volcano, before
your eyes
As the blood, of his very being is
trapped in danger
But faith, yes, his faith in God never dies.

He asks himself, being perplexed,
confused but not amused

"When is the liberation of my people,
From the chains of oppression,
humiliation, rejection
Confusion, suppression acquires global attention?
Is this the task set before me,
To liberate my people from the
bondage of slavery?"

Join me, in force, number and solidarity
Empowering and materializing the
dream before me
For the sacrifices, of our ancestors,
must not go unrecognized,
Ignored or denied despite them being dehumanized.

Hold high the torch of perseverance
and dedication
Of a people, a dream and a struggle
common to our nation
For proud, strong and united we must be
To overcome the hardships and dry the
tears of our history;

Let the voice no longer cry in pain
Nor their actions be in vain
For you and I, a new generation,
Has the key to unlock the doors to liberation.

So together we stand, in one accord
To break the back of our tribulation
For generations, yet to come, can record
Upon the pages of civilization
A rebirth to our beloved nation.

MY PEOPLE

My people birth from the loins of Kings, Queens and Warriors
Have been ostracized, victimized, criticized, stigmatized,
Demoralized and marginalized within many borders
But, have surfaced victoriously inspite of being dehumanized.

The diaspora, brought about by the slave trade
Has raped and robbed us of our languages and mores
Compounded by the Africans Holocaust like a switch blade
Beheaded our identity, vision, solidarity and folklores.

The internalization of the scars from this reality
Has stifled and suffocated the breath within us
Manifested division, paranoia and incompability
Despite the power of our heritage, birth from dust.

How often has the venom of slavery
Poisoned and immobilized the fabric of our existence
Constricting our growth and overall imagery
Leaving us confused and lost in suspense?

This is my people, a people of struggles through life
Who slept on the bed of excruciating pain and agony
Drank from the cup of sorrows and strife
And misery and strife were their only company.

Stripped from the arms of the mother-land
Subjected to anguish, tears and pain
Under the fury of the white-man
As they rebelled in vain.

Left upon the footprints of humanity
Is their desire for peace and solidarity
For us, as humans to live as one
Upon this earthly creation!

THE JOURNEY

The enlightenment of a people within a struggle
Burden beneath the fist of oppression,
dehumanization
Is like a beacon of light, within the darkness
of life
That empowers, inspires and provides direction.

My people, the white-man is no longer
your enemy
We have invigorated and perpetuated this
philosophy
That we have lost touch with our own reality
By embracing hypocrisy in the name of solidarity.

Such is my people, within the walls of civilization
Embracing a dream, a hope, a vision
Laid down by our ancestors, like footprints
on the ground
The fabric of our existence, a challenge I
have found.

Yes, the minds and bodies have been
imprisoned and tortured
But, our souls too powerful to be crushed
or touched
So why, disempower ourselves within our culture
With anger, self-hatred and violence so much?

The disassociation, miscommunication and
self-destruction
Fueled, energized and nurtured by our
misconception
Brought upon by political forces and racial
complexions
Undermine dreams of self-autonomy and
self-determination.

The consolidation of our human efforts and
resources
Should bridge the gap and provide our
unification
Not division, intimidation, frustration or
any other forces
Of segregation, degradation, corruption or
disorganization.

Lost in the shuffle, like a needle in a hay-stack
So is my people, inspite of knowledge and
understanding
That ignorance of self is a major stumbling block
That is highly manifested in efforts we are creating.

Knowledge is power, reach out and devour
For today is the hour, my sister, my brother!

VICIOUS MEMORIES

Why am I losing touch with this earth
From the things, people and place of my birth?
Is it because of the tears upon my face
Or the vicious memories of death I can't erase?

The tears, they run like The River Nile
As the hurt compounds the pains inside
For no matter what I can't smile
For I am lost, confused like a little child.

Deaths have dealt me a deadly blow
I am even afraid to pick up the phone
So traumatized and paranoid I go
Scared, perplexed of being alone.

I just can't bear these pains anymore
For my body is so, so numb
Left by deaths upon my door
Transforming me into a squashy gum.

If this is a cup, I must forever drink
Then Lord, "help, help me please,
For there is no strength or thought to think
Within me, on bending knees!"

These children birth from this loin of mine
Are my precious jewels and love divine
Wrenched away from my total being
As I am left confused like a mystery scene.

How often have I long to hold
Their tender bodies so close to me
And tell them ever so bold
Of the love inside and my misery.

Too many nights I lay awake
In pensive, panick thoughts
Wondering what would it take
To bring them closer to my heart?

This emptiness left deep inside
Is like this scar that I can't hide
For no matter what I try to do
Their images take me back to you.

Sometimes, the tears are no comfort
For my grieving soul and heart that care
Though no one sees or feels my heart
Within me, it's too much to bear.

Is this the life, I must live alone
Suffering, while pleaing for their company?
Or a test that makes me moan and groan
Being consumed by this pain and agony?

Many times I cry myself to sleep
To desensitize these hurts I feel
But, as I lay me down and weep
There is no escape to what is real.

No burden so great did I have to face
Of tribulations within my stomping ground
And no matter what, I can't erase
Vicious memories of tears upon my tongue.

TWISTED VISION

We claim to be rejected
Neglected, unappreciated
Not to mention obstructed
Under-rated and detested.

What about being dehumanized
Marginalized, victimized
Ostracized, criticized or even stigmatized?

Have we lost our common sense
Due to crimes and violence
Compounded by our arrogance
And aggravated by ignorance?

We often manifest our stupidity
In light of this harsh reality
That we are forever in search of equality
But, simultaneously undermine our objectivity.

Is it because of our dehumanization or segregation
That we lean towards self-destruction, corruption
Or are we lost in frustration
Or even our sense of direction?

Stop, these are not the fabric of our existence!
We are strong, full of energy and intelligence!
So, why subject ourselves to humiliation
By fueling and empowering these
misconceptions?

Our ancestors' struggles and pains all left a trace
Of the hardships, humiliation and tears we
can't erase
But, with faith-their sweet embrace
They have overcame and brought us a smiling face.

So, let's not embrace hypocrisy in the name of
solidarity
Nor perpetuate old ages of anger and animosity
By misconstruing blackness for stupidity
But, hold fast to yesterday's dreams of prosperity
So together we can build a better, earthly society.

HARSH REALITY

Creeping, slowly, into the secret recesses of the mind
The pages of my memories unfold before my very eyes
How excruciating these images I see
Amidst the terrifying emotions in me!

The pains of hunger flood my soul
So does the zeal to quench this thirst
For many a nights darkness engulf my world
Like a raging fire-shattering dreams as they twirl.

Running in haste, away from these dreams
Bring me back to such harsh realities
When teardrops never cease to be
My friend, my brother and company.

So lost, confuse like a little child
The prayers escape in disaccord
For silence, comfort don't seem to be
Overpowering this world of misery.

Helplessly searching for someone to hold
Results in nothing but more pain and agony
For the truth flashes out so conspicuously
While trying to ease the inner pain in me.

On tossing and turning, like a ship at sea
So is this life that is left in me
Just wandering, will I ever be free
Free, free from such harsh reality?

INNER-PAIN

How burdensome can evil actions be
When taken advantage of by you and me?
"Sorry," can't erase the tears nor pain
That falls upon heart-aches like rain.

Lost in solace and pensive thoughts
Of past and present broken-hearts
Cause teardrops to fall down the cheeks
As lips no longer seem to speak.

How vicious and insensitive one can be
Of creating such world of inner misery
As words so cold and sharp like ice
Cut through the heart with a brutal slice.

How distasteful and anguishing this pain inside
Camouflage by sentiments one tries to hide
Torturing, rupturing this very being
As memories ignite such gruesome scene.

No words of comfort or sweet embrace
Can wipe away this bitter taste
That lingers upon this teary face
While running away in anger and haste.

THE BLACKNESS!

The blackness in me
Is not ashamed to be
A part of our history
Where cometh my dignity!

Call it evil or wicked
Corrupted or crucked
When uprooted and transported
With our history now distorted.

Run to the pyramids and you will see
The height of our technology
The traffic signal and light bulb we use
Not inventions from the blackness abused?

The gas masks use in warfares too
And the peanuts butter sold to you
All birth from the blackness we know
Is hated, rejected and neglected as we grow.

As a people, love and peace we should share
Daily, to over-ride the hatred we fear
To live in love and harmony
Thus, creating a better society.

Is blackness so black, that anger reigns in your soul
Or violence roams like stories untold?
Why detest the ground that I walk
Or even deny the truth that I talk?

The blackness!!

FREEDOM CRIES!

Has slavery taught us to be so blind
To the continuous decapitation of the mind?
How insensitive, vicious and cruel one can be
Of torturing, slaughtering and murdering a family?

Is it the color of our skin
So black, so black that it stains like sin?
Or resistance to the gold, glory, gospel mentality
All tentacles of their imperialistic identity?

The manifestation of the waves of ignorance
Still storms across our existence in arrogance
And enslaves not the body anymore
But the mind, now chained to the floor.

The blunt of its wrath still lingers on
Like an unstoppable train blows its horn
Ravishing, destroying and demolishing
"Relationships" as Willy Lynch said in everything.

But, from the mountain top or valleys below
Those beacons of lights forever glow
For even in the darkest days
That glow of hope never fails.

The racial tensions and anger inside
Forever rage on, so deep and wide
And as the heat intensifies
So the voice of freedom cries!

15

REMINISCING!

Was it yesterday, I heard him say
"Our past was like a scarry day,
Full of anger, hatred and fear
Not to mention, endless tear.

The demarcation between black and white
Was the difference between day and night
For as the stars did shine so bright
In our lives there was no light.

The blood of our ancestors flooded the streets
And houses burnt down where we use to meet
Access to education and transport were denied
And for freedom of speech, many had died.

The places we went were black in everyway
Antiracial intermingling was the law of the day
For though the rain fell on us all
There was a different god upon whom we called.

Were these vicious, morral thoughts
Brought to life through actions and deeds
Or pain and hatred down deep in hearts
That spreaded so wild, wild like those weeds?

Many a night, on bending knees
Comfort of prayer didn't help or ease
The forever longing to be free
Free from this racial misery.

TRANSFORMATION!

The underdevelopment of our African Society
By the fist and fury of the Europeans
And their imperialistic and colonialistic mentality
Resulted in the diaspora of a people and nation.

The instruments of divide and conquer
Fueled by the racial hatred and anger
Were birthing ground for thirst and hunger
Not to mention, endless murder.

The precious jewels like diamond and gold
Powered the venom of territorial exploitation
That poisoned tribal infrastructures of old
And climaxed into this racial oppression.

The military alliance of power and might
Subdued the body and the mind
But, not the soul when in fight
For the quest of freedom we longed to find.

The transmigration of that force within
Propelled us forward to aim for the moon
And despite our color be classed as sin
"Stars" we have become, so early, so soon.

Our knowledge has taken us to space and back
Even as doctors we have stopped heart-attacks
And in sports-excellence is our name
So we are proud of the blackness and the fame.

So thanks to the oppression of slavery days
Which has transformed us from ashes to gold
For even with these positive-ways
Our true history is yet to be told.

UNITE!

The voice of freedom has cried
Beyond the walls of agony and pain
For though many lives have died
A dream of that nature is yet to gain.

Stifled and shackled in chains of slavery
Utterances of moaning spoke on our behalf
How dismal was our strength of bravery
When freedom of speech was transformed to cough?

Throughout the years a dream was surfaced
That one day, black and white would be hand-in-hand
And the black man will not be judged by skin nor face
But, the content of his character-as a black- man.

Today, we hear that voice once again
Crying out from the wilderness of our souls
As black and white now converge in pain
In seeking mutual goals.

As we surface from the walls of arrogance
Once considered the blackness of our stupidity
We no longer hide behind the curtain of ignorance
But ride on the waves of self-integrity.

So, let us unite, despite color or creed
For the struggles rain down
Not just on the weed
But, all those upon the ground.

The greatest nation upon God's earth
Is led by a black-man, of Africa's birth
And the voice that cries, crieth for freedom
Not just for blacks nor whites but,
For all, within this kingdom.

SOCIAL TRANSITION!

The electrifying voice rains down like thunder
Mobilizing a people to thought and action
To overcome this socio-economic and political blunder
That has stagnated and under-rated this nation.

The racial struggles have overshadowed the light of hope
For many years within the veins of our system
But, no longer, as a people, can we cope
With the bondages of slavery and repucussions of them.

The mind is no longer enslaved to the walls of slavery
But, liberated to soar and explore new horizons
With a new found sense of bravery
Not to dehumanize but, inspire and create positive visions.

The white-man is no longer our enemy
But, catalyst to change, old anger and rage
And change the way we think and act as a family
Thereby empowering our color of skin and image.

May the beds of agony, upon which teardrops fell
Be the breeding ground for unity and dignity
And our stance be as strong as the trees that tell
Of our courage and strength while being lynched;
    A harsh and gruesome reality.

The scars on our backs, from the cat-of-nine tails
Are foot-prints of our journey, journey to fame
Across the Atlantic, so vicious, so treacherous, so many sails
    In obliterating old hatred and shame.

REDEMPTION!

The inflammatory, electrifying and invigorating speech
So eloquently, forcefully and confidently delivered
Inspired, motivated and activated regions within reach
To soar like great eagles without been tired.

The internal transformation of will to might
Empowered, energized and propelled the nation
With a force and vision, so bright as the light
That shines by day and by night
With one, earthly, resolution.

So intelligently mesmerizing, were the words of choice
As the sound of freedom resonated from his voice
And held together that sweet embrace
Of a people and a nation upon his face.

How awesome it was to see our commander in chief
Standing so tall and proud-as a black-man
Delivering such momentous speech-that's never so brief
And impregnated with wisdom and knowledge to understand.

His great sense of humour and profound humility
Manifested his strength, power and authority
And as he succinctly and categorically disclosed his goals
Rivers of happiness flooded our souls.

That dream of yesterday is today's reality
When the black-man is no longer judged by the color of his skin
Nor put to shame because of his identity
But, now exalted due to the content of his character;
Once equated to that of sin.

DREAMERS!!

Our ancestors' bones buried beneath the earth
Far, far from the place of their birth
Spoke of their struggles, sufferings and deaths
Such actions can't be fathomed without a breath.

Like footprints on the pages of history
So are these dreamers of a harsh reality
That pioneered our pathway from sorrow
To a better and brighter tomorrow!

Institutions of higher learning weren't afforded us
But, through determination, humiliation and negotiation
It was transformed to a "must."
And Ms. Rosa Parks' stance revolutionized public transportation.

Shirley Chisholm's entrance as the first black woman to congress,
Paul Robesson, renowned black activist against injustice
And the Tuskegee Airmen and The Triple Nickles all laid to rest
In the fight for socio-economic and political liberation, during their service.

The list goes on, like The River Nile:
Harriet Tubman and William Still, pioneers of the underground railroad,
Almena Lomax, founder of the L.A's news paper; that sometimes bring a tear or smile
And Malcolm "X", a social activist been shot in a crowd.

The contributions made to our history's legacy
As Dr. Martin Luther King's dream of the unification of black and white,
Would one day be, which was so far to see
And the black-man not judged by color of skin but, character
The depth of such intangible, rare and valuable value within!

So rise my people
And be transformed by the renewal of your minds
Not the color of your skin
But be empowered within!

21

SOCIAL CRISIS!

The inner-circle in which we live
Shows signs and remnants of yesterday
When in chain of misery and submerge in pain
Our souls cry out with a lot to say.

How territorial and arrogant we get
In allegiance to a color, creed or code
And even if death does beset
The rage and anger fuel our actions' mode.

There is no freedom of peace anymore
In spite of the spiritual family values learnt
That roamed in our lives, as children on the floor
With the lessons now thrown away and burnt.

Our distance of respect and courteousness
    to each other
Is as far as the west is from the east
And the hatred, jealousy that flood our brother
Bring out the human-animal like a beast.

The blood of innocent people flow along
    the streets
Where prayers once held and seniors meet
And no longer can the children play
Without being fearful night and day.

Is the social infrastructure of law and order
The mechanism perpetuating these crimes
    and violence
That lead to torture, rape and murder
And rain down on us like a plague of pestilence?

Is the blackness in us so evil as sin
Or is it the scars from slavery within?
Are we still chained to the bondage of slavery
That mentally, now, we are weak and lack
    of bravery?

Stand firm, my friends
And transform yourselves for the fight
Not as robots but as men
Who whether the storm despite the plight!

PERPLEXITY

What fate in life
 Do I face
Confronting this strife
 That I trace?

The thoughts haunt my very being
So daily like a mystery scene
And yet confuse, like a little child
Teardrops fall down, so free and wild.

How empty do I feel so often
Beneath this burdensome trend of thought
Is it the fear of a darkened-coffin
Or that of a lonely, broken-heart?

Visions roam before my eyes
Of troubling days and black, black skies
As if to say," miseries will fall,
Like raindrops on a broken wall."

How gruesome and dismal can my life be
When hopes and dreams seem to disappear
Leaving me with such agony
As my flesh seems to rip and tear.

The anguishing pain upon my face
 Speaks of hidden aches inside
For as I crumble and crumble like waste
 These tears I cry, I can't hide.

No pain has filled this heart of mine
Like the blows of death, I do find
So sour, so vicious, so excruciating
As it tears and rips this being within.

Oh, how these scary thoughts flood my sleep
Of ghostly figures-scream and weep
 Oh, how venomous is it sting
On paralyzing this earthly, human-thing.

 So often, on bending knees
 Prayers, they raise up to the sky
And yet, puzzled, beneath these trees
 No answers have been given why.

23

DEFORMATION

The poem you are about to read
May not be welcoming to the ear
For the subjugation of women to that of an object
And a sex object at that poisons the world we share.

Among the deadliest arsenal of man's demise
Is the utilization and implementation of "pussypolytricks"
The capitalization of such has dehumanized
The identity, integrity and dignity of women in my eyes.

The marketability of such valuable commodity
Whether legalize, illegalize or otherwise
Greatly transcends the periphery of our moral society
Fueling crimes of enormous proportion and perplexity.

Such lethal weapon infiltrates any given situation
In a conniving, deceitful and snakelike manner
That manifests many faces leading to destruction
Via seduction, passion, humiliation or incarceration.

The strongest of men have fallen victim
To this weak but, yet powerful vessel
So instrumental in undermining and accomplishing
The just objective in everything and anything.

The sexual exploitation is further perpetuated
By the economic power, growth and acquisition
Despite the applicators themselves being impacted
Because of interpretations of such actions.

Despite intelligence, socio-economic or political status
The upward mobility of this species is the impetus
That drives and is attributed to sexual objectivity
That over shadows the inward beauty.

So be that of substance and class
Not a toy or rug to be tossed!
Once used, abused or misused
Like the earth beneath your shoes.

DEATH'S SCAR

Like a ton of bricks it fell on me
A thought, a pain, a memory
So rough, so rough, so rough as can be
The oppression and exploitation of my ancestry.

Despite the tears and pains inside
No place of comfort or place to hide
For the emptiness that floods my soul
Forever haunts me, like this frigid cold.

I can still feel the pain
For the lost, of our love ones, is never so brief
For the teardrops they fall and fall like rain
That compounds the hurt, pain and grief.

Sleepless nights of anguish and pain
Became my friends, beneath the rain.
How excruciating is this feeling within
That scars my soul, so black as sin?

No words of comfort or warm embrace
Can wipe away the pain I face
For the tears they linger upon my tongue
As I lay helplessly, without a sound.

TROUBLED-THOUGHTS

How powerful are these thoughts of mine
Awakening the submerged pains inside
As hidden captive, I can't find
The inner-peace, despite I tried.

Questioning eyes in search of sight
Bear witness to this misery and plight
For even with my hands unfold
Answers to prayers returned so cold.

Like troubled waters, beneath this bridge
So is my life, as it rocks and rolls
Along this darkened, distant hedge
And crashes into many folds.

The anguishing looks upon my face
Leap from the wilderness of my soul
Where teardrops never seem to trace
The birth-place of heart-achs untold.

Meandering in this valley, with a thirsty tongue
No light of hope ever thus shines
For the stumbling blocks they fall upon
My life, my world combine.

APARTHEID!

Synonym for segregation or to separate the identity
A harsh, cruel and venomous reality
Institutionalize racism of poor and
marginalized blacks
Roam on the waves of social structures
like heart-attacks!

Ammunitions usage to suppress
antigovernment's protestors
In the wave of black empowerment and
self-realization
Is further fuel by unemployment and racist masters
Militarily, articulating the pain of the
poor to frustration.

The furious demonstrations against the
conspicuous injustices
Are consequences of these phenomena
escalating into crises
And paralyze the infrastructures of development
Inspite of been institutionalized by the
government.

The racial inequality been compounded by poverty
Accentuate government's potent symbol of cruelty
To dehumanize, victimize and ostracize
A people, a nation full of visions to realize.

The killing of people and creation of a blood-bath
Give birth to the escalation of anger and wrath
And the supression of their determination
to self-autonomy
Invariable becomes the bedroom of
social disharmony.

The temerity to organize and protest
against those structures
Fall short of the mandates of the political
infrastructures,
Thereby angering residents belief in
government's ability
To improve, better and enhance their society.

As the raging hatred floods their souls
Turmoil of anguish foster their goals
To empower and free themselves from
bondage of oppression,
Opposition, victimization and murderation.

Is the global community so blind, blind to see
Like it did to Rwanda and Darfur of such
gruesome reality
Or its socio-economic and political interests
Are not there to its best?

"Mepa's poems are very interesting, insightful and thought provoking. I wish him all the best and luck in his journey."

Tracy Zimmerman, Court Services Assistant 111.

"The content is very rich and pregnant with meaning."

Chris Iwu, Management Consultant

"Reading these poems, I am moved with emotions. How eloquently you narrate the stories of our people. We are a beautiful people with a rich history and culture that need to be shared. Thank you for reminding us that from what we have come through, we can do and achieve any and everything. I really enjoyed reading this."

Monica Rose Sweeney, Administrative Assistant

"These poems speak with such a powerful voice, that it brings tears to us. However, we are uplifted to learn of the struggles, sacrifices and the great achievements of our ancestors. Consequently, we endorse these writings with the cover as a gift to our ancestors and our African Heritage."

Robert Garcia, "Prax," and **Kimberly Tilmon Garcia**, wife, of Blessed- Love Owners and Managers

"These elegant writings truly reflect the struggles and achievements of a strong, spiritually and empowered people!

Irvin Lackey, Judicial Assistant

"I was sincerely touched by the poignant words of Mr. Murray. His ability to connect to his ancestry is indicative of his artistic ability. Further, his visceral understanding of the difficulties of modern racial identification are exemplary, to say the least. A great piece of work!"

Craig Kirwood, Attorney-at-law.

"Mr. Murray is an inspiration! I am very pleased to have met him and I am very encouraged by his contribution to our world community. The depth of his heart, knowledge, spirit and desire to communicate the journey of his people are highly amplified in these writings. I am looking forward to the publication of his book of which I plan on sharing throughout The United States, Central and South America."

Gordon Turner, Attorney-at-law

Printed in the United States
By Bookmasters